Alphabet Practice

Write the missing uppercase letters or lowercase letters.

a   B   C   d

E   f   g   H

i   J   K   I

M   n   o   P

q   R   S   t

U   v   w   X

Y

z

Aa, Bb, Cc

Write the alphabet neatly.
Write uppercase letters and lowercase letters.

Starts the Same

Circle the three pictures in each row that begin with the same sound.

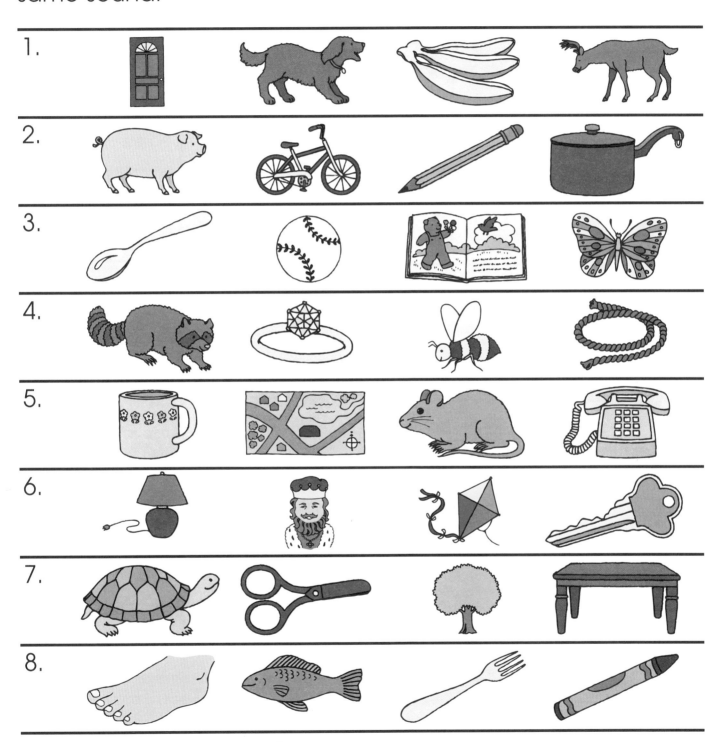

What Sound Does It Begin With?

Look at the picture. What sound does it begin with?
Fill in the circle next to the matching letter.

○ b
○ f
● s

5. ○ p
○ t
○ v

10. ○ k
○ f
○ r

15. ○ b
○ r
○ f

1. ○ m
○ k
○ d

6. ○ y
○ b
○ g

11. ○ n
○ z
○ t

16. ○ j
○ d
○ h

2. ○ g
○ f
○ z

7. ○ z
○ m
○ h

12. ○ w
○ p
○ y

17. ○ l
○ s
○ v

3. ○ h
○ l
○ n

8. ○ f
○ j
○ l

13. ○ v
○ b
○ k

18. ○ r
○ n
○ b

4. ○ r
○ w
○ j

9. ○ n
○ s
○ p

14. ○ m
○ g
○ n

19. ○ b
○ r
○ g

Fun With Blends

Write the missing blend: **bl**, **cl**, **fl**, **gl**, **pl**, or **sl**.

1.  ____ ock

2.  ____ obe

3.  ____ ag

4.  ____ ant

5.  ____ ock

6.  ____ ue

7.  ____ ide

8.  ____ ute

9.  ____ ower

10.  ____ oud

11.  ____ anet

12.  ____ ed

13. ____ anket

14.  ____ own

15.  ____ ove

16. ____ ane

Which Blend?

Write the missing blend: **br**, **dr**, **gr**, **pr**, or **tr**.

1. Things that go

____ ain

____ uck

____ actor

2. Food

____ apes

____ ead

____ etzel

3. Colors

____ een

____ own

____ ay

4. Things outside

____ ee

____ idge

____ ound

5. Instruments

____ umpet

____ um

____ iangle

6. People

____ andma

____ other

____ ince

Puzzle Fun

Fill in the blank with **ch**, **sh**, or **th**.
Find and circle each word in the puzzle.

1.  ___ air

2.  ___ ell

3. **3** ___ ree

4.  ___ est

5. ___ eep

6.  ___ oe

7.  ___ ain

8.  ___ umb

s	k	u	c	s	h	o	e	t
h	c	t	h	u	m	b	p	h
e	h	o	c	h	e	s	t	r
l	a	s	h	e	e	p	y	e
l	i	m	p	d	o	n	e	e
f	n	u	g	c	h	a	i	r

Silent Consonants

These words all have silent consonants.
Color the boxes of the consonants you do not hear.

1. w r i t e

2. c l i m b

3. l i g h t

4. w a l k

5. i s l a n d

6. k n e e

7. s i g n

8. s n o w

9. s c i e n c e

10. g h o s t

Which Vowel?

Write the missing short vowel: **a**, **e**, **i**, **o**, or **u**.

1.  p __ g

2.  c __ p

3.  n __ st

4.  p __ t

5.  b __ g

6. d __ ck

7.  p __ n

8. sh __ ll

9.  h __ t

10. ch __ ck

11.  f __ n

12.  r __ g

13.  m __ p

14.  fr __ g

15.  b __ d

16. l __ ck

Step by Step

1. Short **a** words: Draw a ○ around the pictures.
2. Short **e** words: Draw an **X** on the pictures.
3. Short **i** words: Draw a □ around the pictures.
4. Short **o** words: Draw a △ around the pictures.
5. Short **u** words: Draw a _____ under the pictures.

Silent E Words

Write the missing long vowel **a**, **i**, **o**, or **u** in the first blank. Write the silent **e** in the second blank.

1.  m __ c __

2.  c __ k __

3.  b __ n __

4. b __ k __

5. f __ v __

6. fl __ t __

7. r __ p __

8.  g __ m __

9. 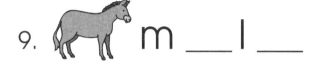 m __ l __

10. r __ k __

11. f __ c __

12. h __ s __

13. h __ m __

14. k __ t __

Long Vowels

Write the missing long vowel: **a**, **i**, **o**, or **u**.
Circle the silent **e**.

1. Play

sk ___ te

sl ___ de

j ___ ke

2. Animals

___ pe

m ___ le

sn ___ ke

3. School

gl ___ be

t ___ pe

c ___ ge

4. Home

ph ___ ne

v ___ se

kn ___ fe

5. Fruits

gr ___ pe

l ___ me

pr ___ ne

6. Names

M ___ ke

R ___ se

L ___ ke

It Takes Two

Match each word to its picture.
Underline the two vowels in each word.

1. p<u>ai</u>l

9. goat

2. boat

10. rain

3. fruit

11. coat

4. chain

12. soap

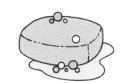

5. tree

13. seal

6. sheep

14. tie

7. train

15. stream

8. pie

16. road

Y Can Be a Vowel

In the word *funny,* the **y** makes the long **e** sound.
In the word *dry,* the **y** makes the long **i** sound.
Say each word. Write it under the correct vowel sound.

baby   cry   fly   party

fry   story   city   sky

y sounds like e

y sounds like i

Rhyming Words

Circle the three pictures in each row that rhyme.

Rhyme Time

Write the rhyming word that matches the picture.

1.  wet _____

2.  long _____

3.  pink _____

4.  hot _____

5.  wee _____

6.  big _____

7.  steel _____

8.  numb _____

9.  bright _____

10.  small _____

11.  cool _____

12. white _____

Twins

Write the word from the fishtank that has the same meaning.

large	begin	high	nice
earth	under	noisy	shut

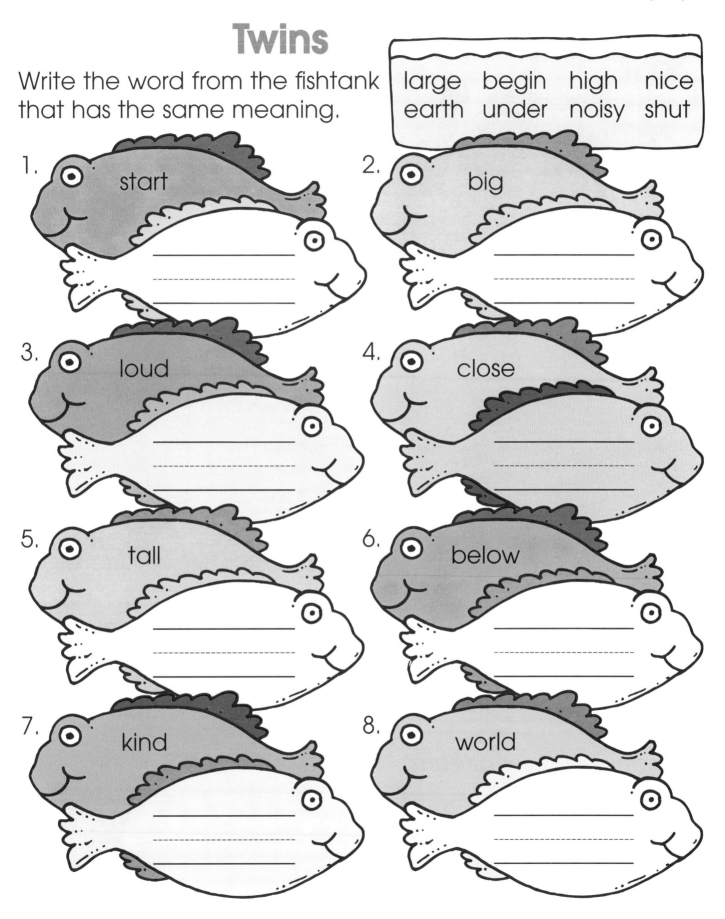

1. start _____

2. big _____

3. loud _____

4. close _____

5. tall _____

6. below _____

7. kind _____

8. world _____

Working Animals

paths
road   hard
find   lift   sea   over

Write the word that means the same as the word in **purple** print.

1. Pets cheer you up if you have had a **difficult** day.

_____

2. Rescue dogs **locate** people who are lost.

_____

3. Seeing Eye dogs help blind people cross the **street**.

_____

4. Elephants can **raise** heavy logs with their trunks.

_____

5. Camels carry people **across** the warm desert.

_____

6. Llamas carry bags up steep mountain **trails**.

_____

7. Seals and other **ocean** animals do tricks.

_____

Up and Down

Match each word to its opposite.

happy •	• off	friend •	• none
fast •	• sad	all •	• out
on •	• right	never •	• enemy
girl •	• slow	in •	• always
left •	• her	add •	• little
come •	• boy	big •	• above
his •	• last	below •	• subtract
yes •	• no	light •	• dark
first •	• go	day •	• bad
long •	• short	good •	• night
more •	• hurt		
help •	• less		

Your Amazing Body

Write the word that is the opposite of the word in **green** print.

loud	left
cold	asleep
big	out

1. Your brain tells your body what to do when

   _____

   you are **awake** and _____ .

   _____

2. Your **right** eye and _____ eye see different things.

   _____

3. Your ears can hear _____ and **soft** sounds.

4. Your skin lets you feel whether things are

   _____

   hot or _____ .

   _____

5. Your body has _____ and **little** bones.

6. Your chest moves when you breathe

   _____

   in and _____ .

20

Animal Words

Use a word from each wing to make one compound word for each picture.

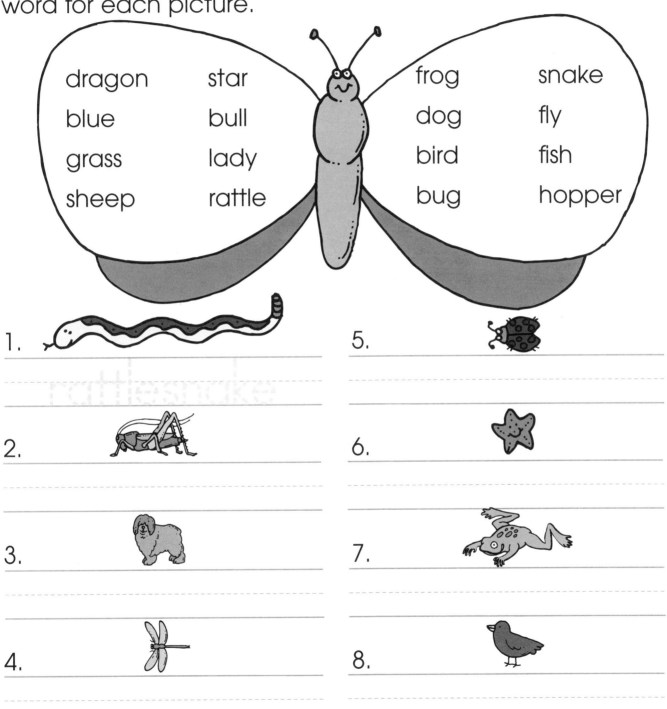

dragon	star	frog	snake
blue	bull	dog	fly
grass	lady	bird	fish
sheep	rattle	bug	hopper

1. _rattlesnake_

2. _____

3. _____

4. _____

5. _____

6. _____

7. _____

8. _____

Jenny's Birthday

Circle each compound word.
Write the compound word on the line.

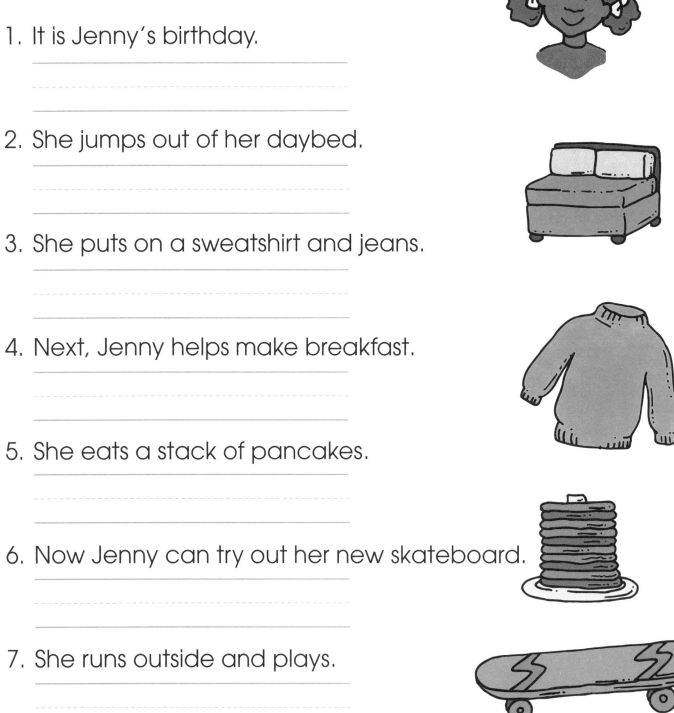

1. It is Jenny's birthday.

2. She jumps out of her daybed.

3. She puts on a sweatshirt and jeans.

4. Next, Jenny helps make breakfast.

5. She eats a stack of pancakes.

6. Now Jenny can try out her new skateboard.

7. She runs outside and plays.

Colorful Robots

1.

Color two robots orange. Color eight robots blue.

2.

Color six robots brown. Color four robots green.

3.

Color nine robots purple. Color one robot yellow.

4.

Color three robots black. Color seven robots red.

5.

Color five robots blue. Color zero robots green.
Leave five robots white.

Bunches of Balloons

Color the balloons.

Color five green.
Color four brown.
Leave three white.

Color ten orange.
Color one black.
Color two yellow.

Color six blue.
Color nine red.

Color eight purple.
Color seven brown.

Find the Word

Fill in the circle next to the matching word.

1. ○ bug
    ○ box
    ○ map

2. ○ house
    ○ sock
    ○ hand

3. ○ purse
    ○ shoe
    ○ plant

4. ○ rake
    ○ coat
    ○ car

5. ○ brick
    ○ boy
    ○ chair

6. ○ dog
    ○ day
    ○ gum

7. ○ drum
    ○ owl
    ○ door

8. ○ floor
    ○ fire
    ○ spoon

9. ○ road
    ○ train
    ○ ring

10. ○ comb
    ○ bike
    ○ bus

11. ○ swim
    ○ gate
    ○ star

12. ○ fall
    ○ fish
    ○ yard

13.  ○ plane
    ○ park
    ○ nose

14.  ○ boat
    ○ hat
    ○ bring

15.  ○ mad
    ○ moon
    ○ jar

16.  ○ heart
    ○ zoo
    ○ him

17.  ○ bird
    ○ queen
    ○ ball

18.  ○ knee
    ○ leaf
    ○ cup

Which Picture?

Read the word. Circle the matching picture.

1. tree

2. book

3. sun

4. dog

5. bath

6. two

7. big

8. food

9. eye

10. sea

11. light

12. rock

13. bell

14. wood

15. wheel

16. game

17. brush

18. rain

19. lion

20. snake

What Does It Say?

Circle the picture that matches each sentence.

1. The boy reads a book.

2. The cat is in the tree.

3. The duck swims in the pond.

4. The girl is sad.

5. The pigs like to dance.

6. The sun is behind a cloud.

Sentence Match-up

Draw a line from each sentence to its picture.

The birds are in the nest.

The mouse has a hat.

The boy is on the slide.

The bear waters the plants.

The girl is playing ball.

It is an apple tree.

The children are swinging.

The pine tree has snow on it.

The fish is in a bowl.

The people are in line.

Let's Go to School

Write the missing words.
Use words from the box.

walk	school
bus	late
car	ride

1. There are many ways to go to _____.

2. Children who live nearby can _____.

3. If they are _____, they need to run.

4. Some children ride the _____.

5. Others like to _____ their bikes.

6. Parents can drive them in a _____.

All Kinds of Helpers

Write the missing words.
Use words from the box.

fires	learn
go	safe
teeth	sick

1. A police officer helps people stay _____ .

2. A firefighter helps stop _____ .

3. A doctor or nurse helps _____ people.

4. A dentist helps people care for their _____ .

5. A bus driver helps people _____ places.

6. A teacher helps children _____ .

A Nature Hike

Read the story. Write the answers.

Tina went on a hike.
She looked for leaves.
She listened to birds.
She smelled some flowers.
She felt a smooth rock.

1. Where did Tina go?

2. What did she look for?

3. What did she hear?

4. What did she touch?

5. What did she use her nose for?

6. What would you do on a hike?

A Fun Trip

Read the story. Write the answers.

Juan is very happy.
He is flying on an airplane.
Juan is going to see his grandma.
She turns 80 years old next week.
Juan will have a fun trip.

1. Whom is Juan going to see?

_____

_____

2. How is he getting there?

_____

_____

3. Who is having a birthday soon?

_____

_____

4. How do you know his grandma lives far away?

_____

_____

5. How does Juan feel about the trip?

_____

_____

6. Where would you like to go on a trip?

_____

_____

Time for Dinner

Which sentence tells the main idea of the whole picture?
Fill in its circle.

- ○ A giraffe likes to eat.
- ○ Trees grow near the giraffe.
- ○ A giraffe eats leaves.

- ○ A squirrel eats nuts.
- ○ A squirrel lives in a tree.
- ○ A squirrel hides nuts in a tree.

- ○ Bear cubs play.
- ○ Mother bear teaches her cubs to hunt for food.
- ○ Bear cubs drink.

- ○ A lizard sits on a rock.
- ○ A lizard catches a bug with its tongue.
- ○ A bug is on a rock.

Summer Fun

Which sentence tells the main idea of the whole picture?
Fill in its circle.

○ The children are selling lemonade.
○ The children made lemonade.
○ The children are outside.

○ Ken likes the pool.
○ Ken likes swimming in the pool.
○ The pool is full of water.

○ Nan has a sister.
○ Nan is playing.
○ Nan and her sister play together.

○ Brad is sleeping.
○ Brad is picking flowers.
○ Flowers need to be watered.

Family Time

Fill in the circle of the sentence that tells the main idea of the story.

Tony likes to help his mom cook.
They make a lot of pasta.
Then they eat a lot of pasta.
Cooking with his mom is fun.

○ Tony loves his mom.
○ Tony likes the food his mom cooks.
○ Tony likes to cook with his mom.

Michelle's dad is teaching her to speak French.
She can say *hello* and *goodbye*.
She can count to 10.
She can say *please* and *thank you*.

○ Michelle can count to 10 in French.
○ Michelle's dad is teaching her French.
○ French is like English.

Fun With Science

Fill in the circle of the sentence that tells the main idea of the story.

Ashley has a new magnet.
She is finding out what things will stick to it.
She puts it near her pencil.
Nothing happens.
She puts it near a paper clip.
The paper clip sticks to the magnet.

○ Paper clips stick to magnets.
○ Ashley is learning what sticks to magnets.
○ Ashley has a magnet.

The sun is very important to us.
The sun gives off heat.
The sun's heat keeps us warm.
We get light from the sun.

○ The sun is a star.
○ The sun is very important.
○ We get heat from the sun.

What's on the Cover?

Look at the book's cover to answer the questions.

What is the title of the book?

_____

_____

Who is the author of the book?

_____

_____

Who is the illustrator of the book?

_____

_____

A New Cover

Read a book. Make a new cover for the book.
Write the title, the author, and the illustrator.
Draw a picture of your favorite part.

Title

Author

Illustrator

Beginning, Middle, End

Read a story. Draw pictures that show what happened at the beginning, in the middle, and at the end.

Beginning

Middle

End

Title

What Happened?

Read a book. Finish the sentences.

I read the book

At the beginning of the story

In the middle of the story

At the end of the story

My Favorite Character

Think of your favorite book. Draw and label a picture of your favorite character from the book. Then finish the sentence.

Character _____

_____

_____

I liked this character the best because _____

_____

_____

_____

_____

_____

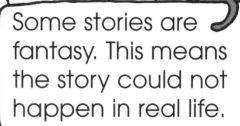

Reality or Fantasy?

Some stories are realistic. This means that the story could happen in real life.

Some stories are fantasy. This means the story could not happen in real life.

Read the sentences. Circle the present if it could really happen. Draw an **X** on the present if it could not happen.

A dog is riding a bike.

The rock is magic.

Eggs come from a chicken.

The cat played with the yarn.

The pig put on his shirt.

The bird built a nest.

Nan went fishing.

The boy rode in a plane.

A fish went to the movies.

The frog drives the bus.

The girl can fly.

The bear ate the fish.

Could It Really Happen?

Some stories are realistic. This means that the story could happen in real life.

Some stories are fantasy. This means the story could not happen in real life.

Read each sentence below. Color the scoop of ice cream blue if it could really happen. Color the scoop of ice cream yellow if it could not happen.

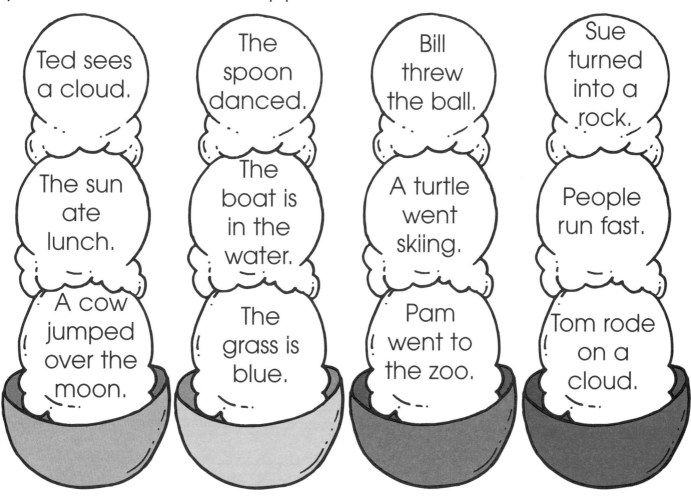

Ted sees a cloud.

The sun ate lunch.

A cow jumped over the moon.

The spoon danced.

The boat is in the water.

The grass is blue.

Bill threw the ball.

A turtle went skiing.

Pam went to the zoo.

Sue turned into a rock.

People run fast.

Tom rode on a cloud.

At the Circus

Write each set of words in ABC order.

1.
lion
horse
elephant

2.
tie
hat
wig

3.
ticket
tent
trapeze

4.
bear
bicycle
balloon

5.
clown
circus
children

6.
peanuts
popcorn
program

Fun at the Park

Write **1**, **2**, and **3** in the circles to put the words in ABC order.

A. ◯ trees
◯ grass
◯ flowers

B. ◯ ducks
◯ fish
◯ pond

C. ◯ stream
◯ waterfall
◯ rocks

D. ◯ kite
◯ ball
◯ jump rope

E. ◯ skates
◯ wheelchair
◯ scooter

F. ◯ dogs
◯ bugs
◯ birds

G. ◯ sand
◯ pail
◯ shovel

H. ◯ seesaw
◯ swings
◯ slide

I. ◯ table
◯ bridge
◯ bench

J. ◯ tires
◯ tree house
◯ tower

K. ◯ skateboard
◯ stroller
◯ bicycle

One or Two?

Draw a line to match each word to its picture.

sock

socks

cats

cat

boat

boats

mouse

mice

roses

rose

baby

babies

numbers

number

foxes

fox

dishes

dish

duck

ducks

eggs

egg

book

books

cars

car

flies

fly

doll

dolls

More Than One

Write the missing words that match the pictures.

1.   hand 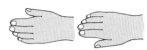 _ _ _ _ _

2.   ball   _ _ _ _ _

3.   _ _ _ _  boxes

4.   star  _ _ _ _ _

5.   tree  _ _ _ _ _

6.   home   _ _ _ _ _

7.   _ _ _   eyes

8.   bird  _ _ _ _ _

Names, Names, Names

Write the names. Begin each with a capital letter.

james

mrs. yee

kyle

mr. larson

anna

sarah

nicole

joseph

ms. lopez

marco

miss ray

ian

You Pick the Name

Write a name in the blank. Begin each with a capital letter.

1. _____ wants to be an astronaut.

2. _____ likes animals.

3. _____ is a very smart dog.

4. _____ and _____ are friends.

5. Mrs. _____ works at our school.

6. _____ is good at art.

7. I know someone named Mr. _____ .

8. My last name is _____ .

9. _____ likes to ride her bike.

10. _____ can sing really well.

All Mixed-up!

Write the words in the correct order to make sentences. The first word in a sentence begins with a capital letter.

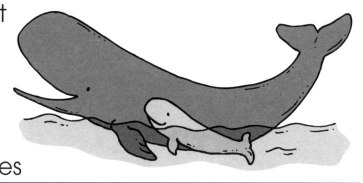

1.   are   big.   Whales

_____

2.   sea.   They   in   the   live

_____

3.   They   swim.   can

_____

4.   not   are   fish.   Whales

_____

5.   mammals.   They   are

_____

6.   drink   whales   milk.   Baby

_____

Kim's Kitten

Write the words in the correct
order to make sentences.
The first word in a sentence
begins with a capital letter.

1. girl.   Kim   a   is

_____

_____

2. very   is   She   smart.

_____

_____

3. wanted   Kim   pet.   a

_____

_____

4. She   kitten.   a   got

_____

_____

5. kitten.   loved   her   Kim

_____

_____

6. with   played   her   Kim   kitten.

_____

_____

A Trip to the Zoo

Read each sentence.
Circle the • if it is a telling sentence.
Circle the ? if it is an asking sentence.

1. We went to the zoo   (•) ?

2. Have you been to a zoo   • (?)

3. We saw lots of animals   • ?

4. The elephants were big   • ?

5. Next, we saw the giraffes   • ?

6. Are you as tall as a giraffe   • ?

7. The monkeys were funny   • ?

8. They chase each other   • ?

9. Do you like to play chase   • ?

10. What is your favorite animal   • ?

11. We liked the sea lions the best   • ?

12. They played in the water   • ?

Planting a Garden

Read each sentence.
Write a • at the end if it is a telling sentence.
Write a ? at the end if it is an asking sentence.

1. We are planting a garden.

2. Have you ever had a garden?

3. First, we need to pull up the weeds

4. Then we will make the soil loose

5. Have you ever seen a worm

6. There are lots of worms in the soil

7. Next, we will plant the seeds

8. What is your favorite vegetable

9. We are planting beans and carrots

10. We will also grow corn and peppers

11. Our garden needs sunshine and water

12. Would you like to plant a garden

My Trip

Think of a trip that you went on. Draw a picture of your favorite part of the trip. Then write a sentence describing it.

Think Back

What is your favorite thing to do at school?
Draw a picture of it. Then write about it.

Nice to Meet You

Yikes! A talking dinosaur just
entered your home.
Write two questions you will ask it.
Then write its answers.

Question

_____

_____

_____

Answer

_____

_____

Question

_____

_____

_____

Answer

_____

_____

A Tasty Tea Party

The Big Bad Wolf is having a tea party.
He's hoping to eat any little pigs that show up!
The party will be held in the deep, dark forest.
It will be on Friday, May 5, at 10 o'clock.

Write the invitation.

Please come
to my tea
party!

_____

Date _____

_____

Time _____

_____

Place _____

_____

Given by _____

Come to My Party!

Pretend you are having a party at your house.
It can be any kind of party you want.
Write the invitation.
Draw pictures to decorate it.

What _____

Date _____

Time _____

Place _____

Given by _____

Folk Tale Thank-you Note

Choose a folk tale you know. Think of how one character helped another. Example:

The woodcutter saved Little Red Riding Hood.

Pretend you are the character who was helped. Write a thank-you note to the other character.

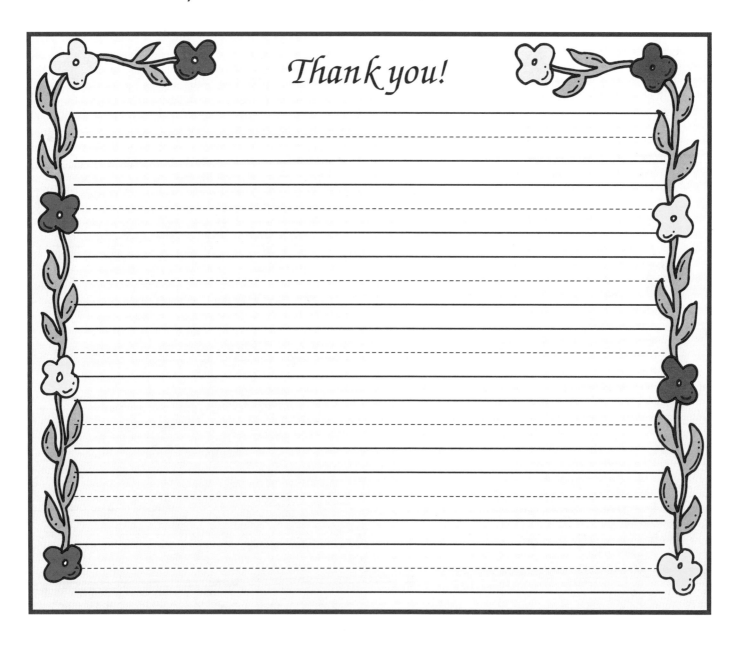

Thank you!

Thank You!

Think of someone who has helped you lately.
Write him or her a thank-you note.

Thank you!

That Doesn't Belong!

Cross out the word that doesn't belong.
Write a new word for each group.

1. **Pets**
   bird
   rabbit
   snow
   fish

2. **School**
   book
   cloud
   pencil
   teacher

3. **Numbers**
   cheese
   seven
   one
   three

4. **Colors**
   box
   black
   yellow
   purple

5. **Family**
   dad
   baby
   tape
   sister

6. **Home**
   bed
   couch
   lamp
   shark

7. **Outside**
   flower
   butterfly
   river
   desk

8. **Food**
   pizza
   six
   salad
   bread

9. **Space**
   rocket
   moon
   bike
   star

Name the Group

Write a title that names each group of pictures.

1. _____

2. _____

3. _____

4. _____

5. _____

6. _____

7. _____

8. _____

Alike and Different

How are a globe and a ball alike?

How are they different?

How are you and a pencil alike?

How are you different?

At the Farm

Use words from the picture for the first two blanks.
Then finish each sentence.

1. A _____ is like a _____ because _____

2. A _____ is like a _____ because _____

3. A _____ is like a _____ because _____

Watch Us Grow

Draw the missing pictures.
Number the boxes **1**, **2**, and **3** to show the order.

chick	egg	hen
child	adult	baby
flower	seedling	seed
egg	frog	tadpole

First, Next, Then, Last

Number the boxes **1**, **2**, **3**, and **4** to show the order.

Busy Bear's Bad Day

Draw a line to match each set of boxes.

Cause		Effect

Busy Bear sleeps late.

He screams.

Busy Bear forgets his lunch.

He misses the bus.

Busy Bear pounds his thumb.

He is hungry.

Busy Bear rides too fast.

His family cheers him up.

Busy Bear feels bad.

He hits a tree.

What Might Happen?

Draw a picture that shows what might happen.

What might happen if your umbrella had a hole?	
What might happen if your teacher got the chicken pox?	
What might happen if you ate too much candy?	

How's the Weather?

Fill in the circle of the sentence that matches the picture.

1. ○ It just rained.
    ○ It just snowed.

2. ○ It is warm.
    ○ It is cold.

3. ○ There is a light breeze.
    ○ There is a strong wind.

4. ○ It is quiet outside.
    ○ It is noisy outside.

5. ○ It is sunny.
    ○ It is cloudy.

6. ○ It is safe to go out.
    ○ It is not safe to go out.

How Do They Feel?

Fill in the circles of the sentences that could match the picture.

1. ○ He is sad.
   ○ He is hurt.
   ○ He is happy.

2. ○ She is lonely.
   ○ She is scared.
   ○ She is surprised.

3. ○ They are mad.
   ○ They are bored.
   ○ They are sleepy.

4. ○ She is sleepy.
   ○ She is bored.
   ○ She is mad.

5. ○ He is lonely.
   ○ He is sad.
   ○ They are all happy.

6. ○ She likes playing alone.
   ○ She is lonely.
   ○ They are all happy.

Sea Life

Use words from the picture for the first two blanks.
Then finish each sentence.

crab
sea gull
dolphin
whale
pelican
starfish
sea horse
shark
squid

1. I would rather **meet** a _____ than a

   _____ because _____

   _____

2. I would rather **be** a _____ than a

   _____ because _____

   _____

A Long Time Ago

Use words from the picture for the first two blanks.
Then finish each sentence.

castle

forest

princess

horse

knight

dragon

cave

1. I would rather **meet** a _____ than a

_____ because _____

_____

_____

2. I would rather **be** a _____ than a

_____ because _____

_____

_____

What's Missing?

Write the missing numbers.

1	2		4					9	
		13				17			
				25					30
			34						
					46				
51									
							67		
								78	
	82								
				95					

Number Chart

Fill in the number chart from 1 to 100.

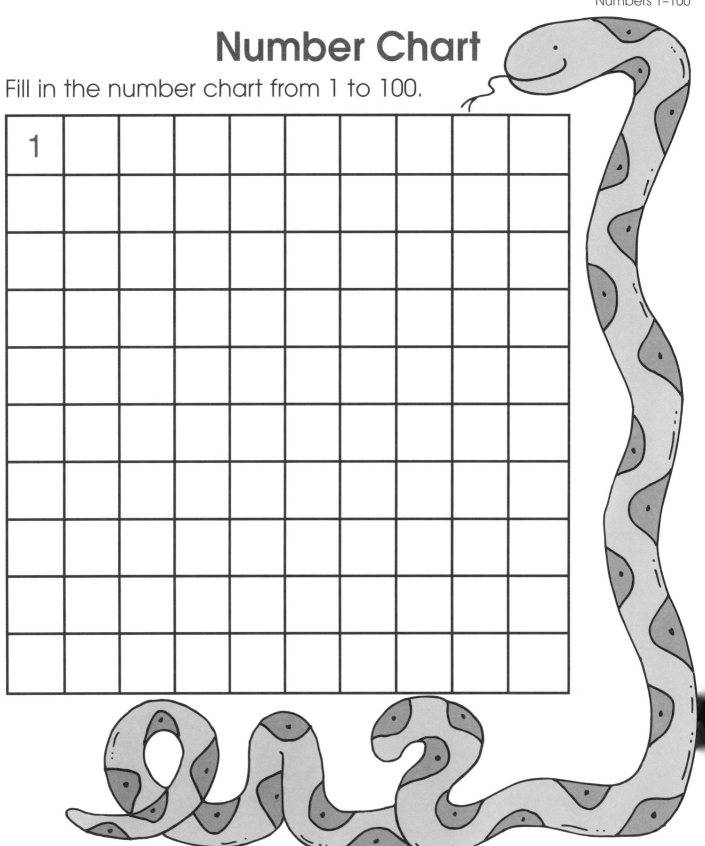

1									

Liftoff!

Count by tens.
Connect the dots from 10 to 100.
Begin at the ★.

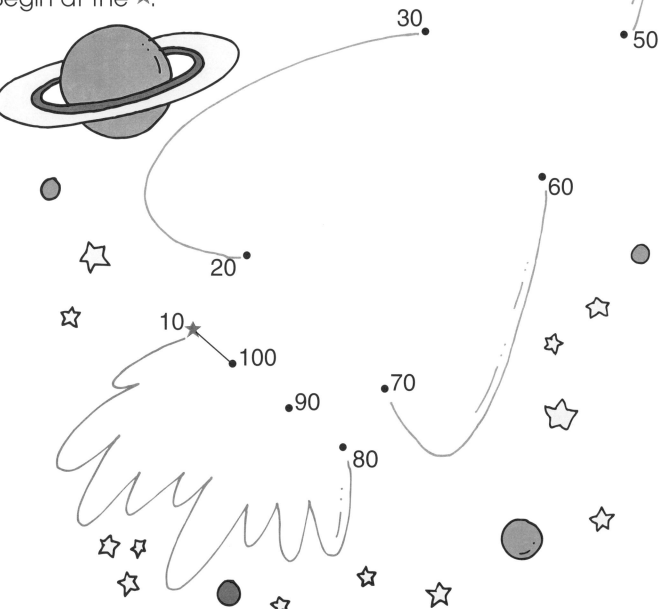

Count by tens. Write the missing numbers.

10, 20, _____, _____, 50, _____, _____, _____, 90, _____

Up, Up, and Away

Count by fives. Connect the dots from 5 to 100.
Begin at the star ★.

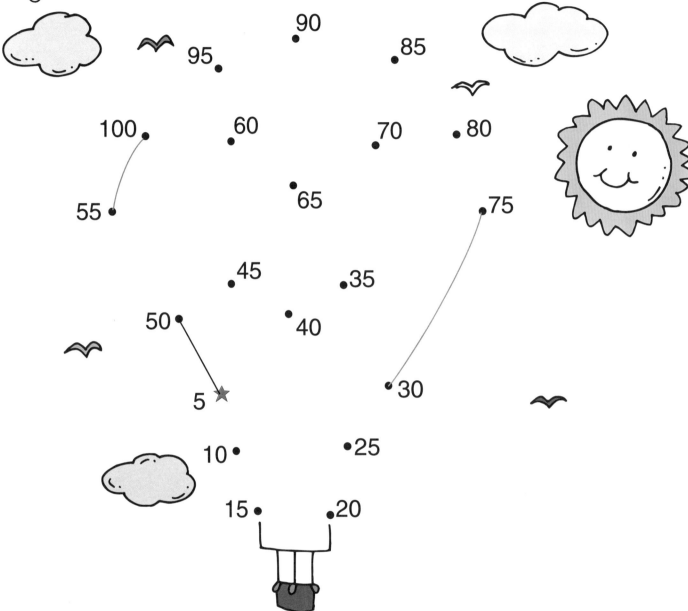

Count by fives. Write the missing numbers.

5, 10, _____, _____, 25, _____, _____, 40, _____, _____, 55,

_____, _____, _____, 75, _____, _____, _____, _____, 100

Alligator Alley

Add.

A.
```
  5      3      6      8      2      9      7      0
+ 2    + 1    + 4    + 9    + 6    + 0    + 7    + 5
```

B.
```
  1      4      5      3      6      8      9      9
+ 1    + 8    + 9    + 6    + 0    + 7    + 9    + 3
```

C.
```
  7      0      1      4      5      3      6      8
+ 3    + 2    + 9    + 4    + 1    + 0    + 6    + 2
```

D.
```
  5      9      0      1      2      4      7      9
+ 8    + 4    + 4    + 6    + 3    + 7    + 5    + 6
```

E.
```
  2      9      3      1
+ 2    + 2    + 8    + 7
```

F.
```
  4      6      7      8
+ 3    + 8    + 9    + 8
```

Play Ball!

Add.

A. 4 + 2 = _____   7 + 6 = _____   8 + 1 = _____

B. 0 + 7 = _____   3 + 5 = _____   9 + 9 = _____

C. 1 + 2 = _____   6 + 3 = _____   7 + 4 = _____

D. 2 + 7 = _____   4 + 1 = _____   0 + 1 = _____

E. 5 + 5 = _____   8 + 6 = _____   6 + 9 = _____

F. 9 + 1 = _____   5 + 7 = _____   4 + 6 = _____

G. 7 + 8 = _____   9 + 5 = _____   1 + 3 = _____

H. 6 + 5 = _____   0 + 8 = _____   2 + 9 = _____

I. 8 + 4 = _____   5 + 0 = _____   5 + 4 = _____

J. 3 + 3 = _____   9 + 8 = _____   3 + 7 = _____

K. 4 + 9 = _____   1 + 5 = _____   3 + 2 = _____

L. 3 + 4 = _____   9 + 7 = _____   8 + 3 = _____

M. 2 + 8 = _____   6 + 2 = _____   3 + 9 = _____

Rainy Day

Add.

A.
$$\begin{array}{r} 15 \\ + 32 \\ \hline \end{array}\quad \begin{array}{r} 30 \\ + 61 \\ \hline \end{array}\quad \begin{array}{r} 64 \\ + 24 \\ \hline \end{array}\quad \begin{array}{r} 58 \\ + 10 \\ \hline \end{array}\quad \begin{array}{r} 20 \\ + 16 \\ \hline \end{array}\quad \begin{array}{r} 19 \\ + 40 \\ \hline \end{array}\quad \begin{array}{r} 32 \\ + 47 \\ \hline \end{array}\quad \begin{array}{r} 40 \\ + 53 \\ \hline \end{array}$$

B.
$$\begin{array}{r} 71 \\ + 21 \\ \hline \end{array}\quad \begin{array}{r} 60 \\ + 39 \\ \hline \end{array}\quad \begin{array}{r} 53 \\ + 43 \\ \hline \end{array}\quad \begin{array}{r} 12 \\ + 76 \\ \hline \end{array}\quad \begin{array}{r} 70 \\ + 10 \\ \hline \end{array}\quad \begin{array}{r} 85 \\ + 13 \\ \hline \end{array}\quad \begin{array}{r} 37 \\ + 50 \\ \hline \end{array}\quad \begin{array}{r} 19 \\ + 60 \\ \hline \end{array}$$

C.
$$\begin{array}{r} 43 \\ + 31 \\ \hline \end{array}\quad \begin{array}{r} 54 \\ + 2 \\ \hline \end{array}\quad \begin{array}{r} 12 \\ + 85 \\ \hline \end{array}\quad \begin{array}{r} 4 \\ + 40 \\ \hline \end{array}\quad \begin{array}{r} 15 \\ + 20 \\ \hline \end{array}\quad \begin{array}{r} 21 \\ + 70 \\ \hline \end{array}\quad \begin{array}{r} 62 \\ + 14 \\ \hline \end{array}\quad \begin{array}{r} 70 \\ + 22 \\ \hline \end{array}$$

D.
$$\begin{array}{r} 53 \\ + 32 \\ \hline \end{array}\quad \begin{array}{r} 36 \\ + 60 \\ \hline \end{array}\quad \begin{array}{r} 20 \\ + 24 \\ \hline \end{array}\quad \begin{array}{r} 41 \\ + 58 \\ \hline \end{array}\quad \begin{array}{r} 22 \\ + 53 \\ \hline \end{array}\quad \begin{array}{r} 43 \\ + 40 \\ \hline \end{array}\quad \begin{array}{r} 30 \\ + 25 \\ \hline \end{array}\quad \begin{array}{r} 14 \\ + 61 \\ \hline \end{array}$$

E.
$$\begin{array}{r} 41 \\ + 45 \\ \hline \end{array}\quad \begin{array}{r} 32 \\ + 62 \\ \hline \end{array}\quad \begin{array}{r} 67 \\ + 22 \\ \hline \end{array}\quad \begin{array}{r} 50 \\ + 27 \\ \hline \end{array}$$

F.
$$\begin{array}{r} 54 \\ + 43 \\ \hline \end{array}\quad \begin{array}{r} 40 \\ + 18 \\ \hline \end{array}\quad \begin{array}{r} 72 \\ + 20 \\ \hline \end{array}\quad \begin{array}{r} 36 \\ + 62 \\ \hline \end{array}$$

Elephant Parade

Add.

A.   23   39   14   57   23   40   32   85
      + 63   + 60   + 64   + 10   + 15   + 50   + 44   + 10

B.   62   61   55   11   12   3   46   25
      + 35   + 8   + 32   + 73   + 42   + 80   + 12   + 34

C.   18   84   30   52   23   47   71   80
      + 80   + 12   + 67   + 40   + 11   + 31   + 20   + 12

D.   50   32   10   73   46   54   10   11
      + 31   + 57   + 55   + 22   + 51   + 40   + 69   + 65

E.   34   61   60   41   87   30   15   60
      + 53   + 11   + 23   + 42   + 12   + 54   + 74   + 36

At the Beach

Subtract.

A.

6	9	3	9	10	10	15	11
−2	−3	−2	−7	−5	−1	−8	−5

B.

12	6	13	7	12	13	8	7
−4	−3	−9	−4	−7	−6	−5	−7

C.

5	14	10	14	8	5	17	6
−1	−6	−8	−5	−8	−0	−8	−5

D.

4	11	11	1	5	11	12	16
−3	−9	−4	−1	−2	−3	−9	−7

E.

8	9	18	9
−2	−1	−9	−4

F.

10	16	10	14
−7	−8	−6	−7

Shining Stars

Subtract.

A. 7 – 3 = ____	14 – 8 = ____	16 – 9 = ____
B. 8 – 7 = ____	11 – 8 = ____	11 – 2 = ____
C. 4 – 2 = ____	15 – 6 = ____	12 – 5 = ____
D. 7 – 6 = ____	13 – 4 = ____	11 – 7 = ____
E. 5 – 3 = ____	17 – 8 = ____	10 – 2 = ____
F. 4 – 4 = ____	13 – 8 = ____	12 – 6 = ____
G. 3 – 0 = ____	10 – 9 = ____	10 – 3 = ____
H. 6 – 1 = ____	12 – 3 = ____	17 – 9 = ____
I. 8 – 4 = ____	18 – 9 = ____	10 – 4 = ____
J. 2 – 2 = ____	15 – 7 = ____	16 – 8 = ____
K. 9 – 6 = ____	14 – 9 = ____	10 – 5 = ____
L. 2 – 1 = ____	12 – 8 = ____	11 – 6 = ____
M. 7 – 2 = ____	14 – 7 = ____	13 – 7 = ____

Spring Flowers

Subtract.

A. 83   69   76   57   96   40   25
    – 63   – 30   – 64   – 10   – 15   – 30   – 14

B. 39   36   41   57   62   85   39
    – 13   – 6   – 40   – 21   – 10   – 50   – 24

C. 81   84   78   99   25   47   83
    – 71   – 40   – 52   – 28   – 23   – 17   – 30

D. 96   87   29   74   98   56   79
    – 90   – 14   – 7   – 32   – 60   – 52   – 25

E. 89   65   98   73   45   91   80
    – 82   – 34   – 43   – 22   – 10   – 31   – 60

Gone Fishing!

Subtract.

A.

91	82	39	48	76	95	47
− 60	− 52	− 28	− 23	− 16	− 30	− 14

B.

49	86	71	59	92	85	39
− 32	− 21	− 51	− 41	− 90	− 72	− 14

C.

67	78	36	90	82	54	76
− 40	− 28	− 32	− 70	− 41	− 10	− 63

D.

68	73	88	49
− 51	− 30	− 4	− 46

E.

59	75	91	62
− 50	− 73	− 81	− 21

F.

84	96	70	35
− 60	− 50	− 50	− 24

Guess and Check

A. Maria and Ann have 7 books in all.
Ann has 3 more than Maria.

How many books does Ann have? _____

How many books does Maria have? _____

B. Lynn and Sam have 9 dinosaurs in all.
Lynn has 1 more than Sam.

How many dinosaurs does Lynn have? _____

How many dinosaurs does Sam have? _____

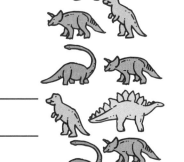

C. Matt and Hannah have 10 cars in all.
Hannah has 2 more than Matt.

How many cars does Matt have? _____

How many cars does Hannah have? _____

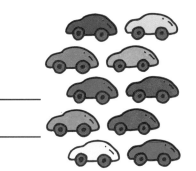

D. Jessica and Danny have 12 cubes in all.
Danny has 4 more than Jessica.

How many cubes does Jessica have? _____

How many cubes does Danny have? _____

Finding a Pattern

A. Mary planted a row of 9 daisies.
She used this color pattern:
orange, purple, purple, orange, purple, purple.
Color the daisies to match the pattern.

How many orange daisies did she plant?_____

How many purple daisies did she plant?_____

B. Paul planted a row of 12 tulips.
He used this color pattern:
red, red, yellow, red, red, yellow.
Color the tulips to match the pattern.

How many red tulips did he plant?_____

How many yellow tulips did he plant?_____

Number Patterns

Find the number pattern.
Write the missing numbers.

A. 43, 44, _____, 46, 47, 48, _____, _____, 51

B. 99, 98, 97, _____, 95, 94, _____, _____, 91

C. 10, 20, _____, 40, 50, _____, 70, _____, 90

D. 5, 10, 15, _____, _____, 30, _____, _____, 45

E. 75, 70, 65, _____, 55, 50, _____, _____, _____

F. 2, 4, 6, _____, 10, _____, 14, _____, _____, 20

G. 1, 3, _____, _____, 9, 11, 13, 15, _____, _____, 21

H. 11, _____, 31, 41, 51, _____, 71, _____, 91, 101

I. 80, 70, _____, _____, 40, _____, _____, 10

J. 30, 28, 26, 24, _____, 20, 18, _____, _____, 12

What Comes Next?

Find the number pattern.
Write the missing numbers.

A. 9, 8, _____, 6, _____, _____, 3, _____, _____, 0

B. 56, 57, 58, _____, 60, 61, _____, _____, _____

C. 10, _____, 30, _____, 50, 60, 70, 80, _____, 100

D. 20, 25, 30, 35, _____, 45, _____, _____, 60, 65

E. 100, 90, 80, _____, 60, _____, _____, 30, _____

F. 0, 2, 4, _____, 8, _____, 12, _____, _____, 18, 20

G. 95, 90, 85, _____, 75, 70, _____, _____, _____

H. 100, 200, _____, 400, 500, 600, _____, _____

I. 1, 3, 5, _____, 9, _____, 13, 15, 17, 19, _____, 23

J. 94, 84, 74, _____, 54, 44, _____, 24, _____, 4

Equal Parts

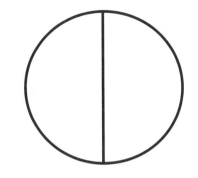

A. Look at the circle.
How many equal parts are there? _____

Write $\frac{1}{2}$ in each part.

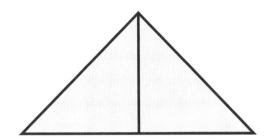

B. Look at the triangle.
How many equal parts are there? _____

Write $\frac{1}{2}$ in each part.

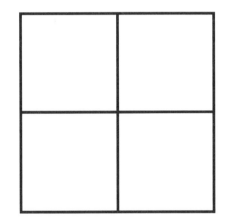

C. Look at the square.
How many equal parts are there? _____

Write $\frac{1}{4}$ in each part.

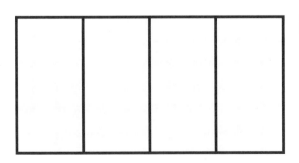

D. Look at the rectangle.
How many equal parts are there? _____

Write $\frac{1}{4}$ in each part.

Wiggly Worms

Measure each worm with your fingertip.
Write how many fingertips long it is.

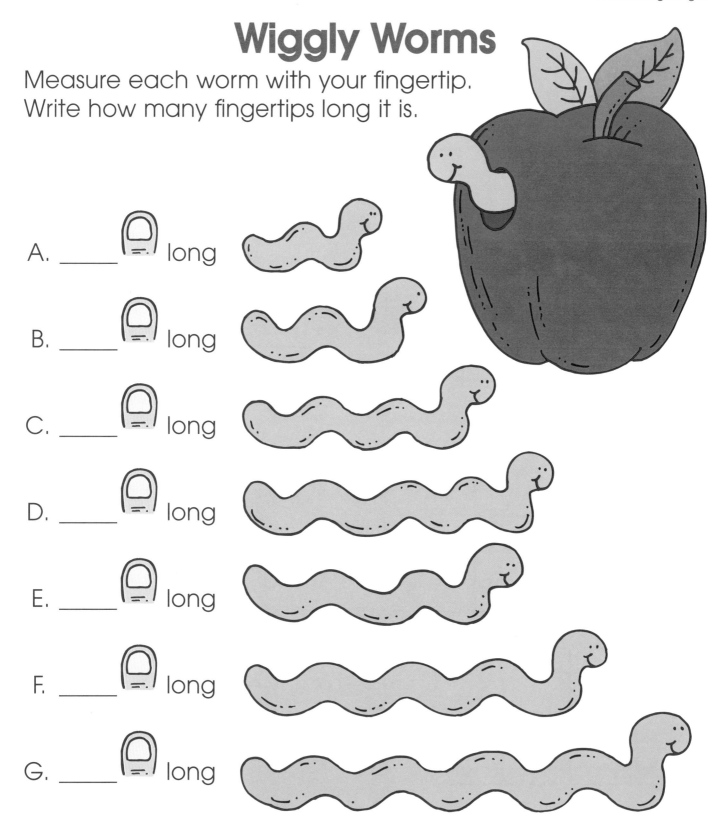

A. _____ 👆 long

B. _____ 👆 long

C. _____ 👆 long

D. _____ 👆 long

E. _____ 👆 long

F. _____ 👆 long

G. _____ 👆 long

How Long Is It?

Fill in the circle next to the correct answer.

A. How many centimeters long is the crayon?
- ○ 6 cm
- ○ 8 cm
- ○ 10 cm

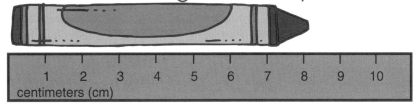

B. How many centimeters long is the pencil?
- ○ 6 cm
- ○ 8 cm
- ○ 10 cm

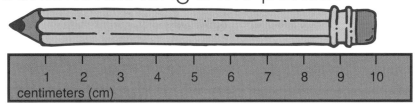

C. How many centimeters long is the sharpener?
- ○ 1 cm
- ○ 2 cm
- ○ 3 cm

D. How many centimeters long is the eraser?
- ○ 1 cm
- ○ 2 cm
- ○ 3 cm

E. How many centimeters long is the paper clip?
- ○ 4 cm
- ○ 6 cm
- ○ 7 cm

What Time Is It?

Write the time.

A. _____ o'clock

B. _____ o'clock

C. _____ o'clock

D. _____ o'clock

E. _____ o'clock

F. _____ o'clock

G. _____ o'clock

H. _____ o'clock

I. _____ o'clock

J. _____ o'clock

K. _____ o'clock

L. _____ o'clock

Clock Match-up

Draw a line from each clock to
the clock with the matching time.

Zoo Animal Graph

Some children voted for their favorite animal.
Read the graph. Answer the questions.

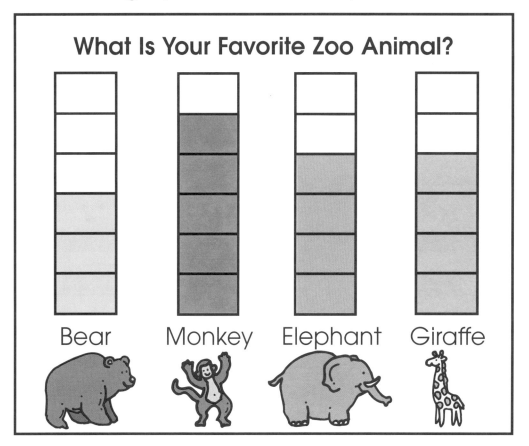

What Is Your Favorite Zoo Animal?

Bear   Monkey   Elephant   Giraffe

1. Which animal did the
   children like the most? _____

2. Which animal did the
   children like the least? _____

3. Which animal got
   the same number of
   votes as the giraffe? _____

Answers

Page Three
1. door, dog, deer
2. pig, pencil, pot
3. ball, book, butterfly
4. raccoon, ring, rope
5. mug, map, mouse
6. king, kite, key
7. turtle, tree, table
8. foot, fish, fork

Page Four
1. k
2. z
3. h
4. j
5. p
6. y
7. m
8. l
9. n
10. r
11. t
12. w
13. v
14. g
15. f
16. d
17. s
18. b
19. r

Page Five
1. cl
2. gl
3. fl
4. pl
5. bl
6. gl
7. sl
8. fl
9. fl
10. cl
11. pl
12. sl
13. bl
14. cl
15. gl
16. pl

Page Six
1. tr, tr, tr
2. gr, br, pr
3. gr, br, gr
4. tr, br, gr
5. tr, dr, tr
6. gr, br, pr

Page Seven
1. ch
2. sh
3. th
4. ch
5. sh
6. sh
7. ch
8. th

Page Eight
1. w
2. b
3. g, h
4. l
5. s
6. k
7. g
8. w
9. c
10. h

Page Nine
1. i
2. u
3. e
4. o
5. u
6. u
7. i
8. e
9. a
10. i
11. a
12. u
13. o
14. o
15. e
16. o

Page Ten
1. bat, flag, hand
2. bell, vest, sled.
3. pig, fish, chick.
4. sock, mop, top.
5. brush, skunk, bus.

Page Eleven
1. i, e
2. a, e
3. o, e
4. i, e
5. i, e
6. u, e
7. o, e
8. a, e
9. u, e
10. a, e
11. a, e
12. o, e
13. o, e
14. i, e

Page Twelve
1. a, i, o
2. a, u, a
3. o, a, a
4. o, a, i
5. a, i, u
6. i, o, u

The silent *e* in each word should be circled.

Page Fourteen
Y sounds like e: baby, story, city, party
Y sounds like i: fry, cry, fly, sky

Page Fifteen
1. bat, hat, cat
2. king, swing, ring
3. well, shell, bell
4. grapes, shapes, apes
5. bug, rug, mug
6. cone, phone, bone
7. brick, chick, stick
8. snake, rake, cake

Page Sixteen
1. net
2. song
3. drink
4. pot
5. bee
6. pig
7. wheel
8. thumb
9. light
10. ball
11. pool
12. kite

Page Seventeen
1. begin
2. large
3. noisy
4. shut
5. high
6. under
7. nice
8. earth

Page Eighteen
1. hard
2. find
3. road
4. lift
5. over
6. paths
7. sea

Page Nineteen
happy, sad
fast, slow
on, off
girl, boy
left, right
come, go
his, her
yes, no
first, last
long, short
more, less
help, hurt
friend, enemy
all, none
never, always
in, out
add, subtract
big, little
below, above
light, dark
day, night
good, bad

Page Twenty
1. asleep
2. left
3. loud
4. cold
5. big
6. out

Page Twenty-one
1. rattlesnake
2. grasshopper
3. sheepdog
4. dragonfly
5. ladybug
6. starfish
7. bullfrog
8. bluebird

Page Twenty-two
1. birthday
2. daybed
3. sweatshirt
4. breakfast
5. pancakes
6. skateboard
7. outside

Page Twenty-five
1. box
2. hand
3. plant
4. car
5. boy
6. dog
7. drum
8. fire
9. road
10. bus
11. star
12. fish
13. plane
14. boat
15. moon
16. heart
17. ball
18. cup

Page Twenty-nine
1. school
2. walk
3. late
4. bus
5. ride
6. car

Page Thirty
1. safe
2. fires
3. sick
4. teeth
5. go
6. learn

Page Thirty-one
1. on a hike
2. leaves
3. birds
4. a smooth rock
5. to smell some flowers

Page Thirty-two
1. his grandma
2. on an airplane
3. Juan's grandma
4. He's taking an airplane.
5. very happy

Page Thirty-three
A giraffe eats leaves.
A squirrel eats nuts.
Mother bear teaches her cubs to hunt for food.
A lizard catches a bug with its tongue.

Page Thirty-four
The children are selling lemonade.
Ken likes swimming in the pool.
Nan and her sister play together.
Brad is picking flowers.

Page Thirty-five
Tony likes to cook with his mom.
Michelle's dad is teaching her French.

Page Thirty-six
Ashley is learning what sticks to magnets.
The sun is very important.

Page Thirty-seven
Tom's Turtle
Emily Clark
Daniel Steele

Page Forty-two
These presents should be circled:
Eggs come from a chicken.
The cat played with the yarn.
The bird built a nest.
Nan went fishing.
The boy rode in a plane.
The bear ate the fish.
The remaining presents should be crossed out.

Answers continued

These scoops should be colored blue:
Ted sees a cloud.
Bill threw the ball.
The boat is in the water.
People run fast.
Pam went to the zoo.
The remaining scoops should be colored yellow.

Page Forty-four
1. elephant, horse, lion
2. hat, tie, wig
3. tent, ticket, trapeze
4. balloon, bear, bicycle
5. children, circus, clown
6. peanuts, popcorn, program

Page Forty-five
A. 3, 2, 1   G. 2, 1, 3
B. 1, 2, 3   H. 1, 3, 2
C. 2, 3, 1   I. 3, 2, 1
D. 3, 1, 2   J. 1, 3, 2
E. 2, 3, 1   K. 2, 3, 1
F. 3, 2, 1

Page Forty-seven
1. hands   5. trees
2. balls   6. homes
3. box   7. eye
4. stars   8. birds

Page Fifty
1. Whales are big.
2. They live in the sea.
3. They can swim.
4. Whales are not fish.
5. They are mammals.
6. Baby whales drink milk.

Page Fifty-one
1. Kim is a girl.
2. She is very smart.
3. Kim wanted a pet.
4. She got a kitten.
5. Kim loved her kitten.
6. Kim played with her kitten.

Page Fifty-two
1. (.)   5. (.)   9. (?)
2. (?)   6. (?)   10. (?)
3. (.)   7. (.)   11. (.)
4. (.)   8. (.)   12. (.)

Page Fifty-three
1. (.)   5. (?)   9. (.)
2. (?)   6. (.)   10. (.)
3. (.)   7. (.)   11. (.)
4. (.)   8. (?)   12. (?)

Page Fifty-seven
Friday, May 5
10 o'clock
Deep, dark forest
Big Bad Wolf

Page Sixty-one
1. snow   6. shark
2. cloud   7. desk
3. cheese   8. six
4. box   9. bike
5. tape
New words will vary. Accept reasonable answers.

Page Sixty-two
Accept reasonable answers.
1. shapes   5. fruit
2. birds   6. flowers
3. tools   7. clothes
4. fish   8. bugs

Page Sixty-five
2, 1, 3
2, 3, 1
3, 2, 1
1, 3, 2

Page Sixty-six
3, 1, 4, 2
2, 4, 3, 1
2, 3, 1, 4
1, 4, 2, 3

Page Sixty-seven
Busy Bear sleeps late.—
He misses the bus.
Busy Bear forgets his lunch.—
He is hungry.
Busy Bear pounds his thumb.—He screams.
Busy Bear rides too fast.—
He hits a tree.
Busy Bear feels bad.—
His family cheers him up.

Page Sixty-nine
1. It just rained.
2. It is cold.
3. There is a strong wind.
4. It is noisy outside.
5. It is sunny.
6. It is not safe to go out.

Page Seventy
1. He is sad. He is hurt.
2. She is scared. She is surprised.
3. They are mad. They are bored.
4. She is sleepy. She is bored.

5. He is lonely. He is sad.
6. She likes playing alone. They are all happy.

Page Seventy-seven
A. 7, 4, 10, 17, 8, 9, 14, 5
B. 2, 12, 14, 9, 6, 15, 18, 12
C. 10, 2, 10, 8, 6, 3, 12, 10
D. 13, 13, 4, 7, 5, 11, 12, 15
E. 4, 11, 11, 8
F. 7, 14, 16, 16

Page Seventy-eight
A. 6, 13, 9   H. 11, 8, 11
B. 7, 8, 18   I. 12, 5, 9
C. 3, 9, 11   J. 6, 17, 10
D. 9, 5, 1   K. 13, 6, 5
E. 10, 14, 15   L. 7, 16, 11
F. 10, 12, 10   M. 10, 8, 12
G. 15, 14, 4

Page Seventy-nine
A. 47, 91, 88, 68, 36, 59, 79, 93
B. 92, 99, 96, 88, 80, 98, 87, 79
C. 74, 56, 97, 44, 35, 91, 76, 92
D. 85, 96, 44, 99, 75, 83, 55, 75
E. 86, 94, 89, 77
F. 97, 58, 92, 98

Page Eighty
A. 86, 99, 78, 67, 38, 90, 76, 95
B. 97, 69, 87, 84, 54, 83, 58, 59
C. 98, 96, 97, 92, 34, 78, 91, 92
D. 81, 89, 65, 95, 97, 94, 79, 76
E. 87, 72, 83, 83, 99, 84, 89, 96

Page Eighty-one
A. 4, 6, 1, 2, 5, 9, 7, 6
B. 8, 3, 4, 3, 5, 7, 3, 0
C. 4, 8, 2, 9, 0, 5, 9, 1
D. 1, 2, 7, 0, 3, 8, 3, 9
E. 6, 8, 9, 5
F. 3, 8, 4, 7

Page Eighty-two
A. 4, 6, 7   H. 5, 9, 8
B. 1, 3, 9   I. 4, 9, 6
C. 2, 9, 7   J. 0, 8, 8
D. 1, 9, 4   K. 3, 5, 5
E. 2, 9, 8   L. 1, 4, 5
F. 0, 5, 6   M. 5, 7, 6
G. 3, 1, 7

Page Eighty-three
A. 20, 39, 12, 47, 81, 10, 11
B. 26, 30, 1, 36, 52, 35, 15
C. 10, 44, 26, 71, 2, 30, 53
D. 6, 73, 22, 42, 38, 4, 54
E. 7, 31, 55, 51, 35, 60, 20

Page Eighty-four
A. 31, 30, 11, 25, 60, 65, 33
B. 17, 65, 20, 18, 2, 13, 25
C. 27, 50, 4, 20, 41, 44, 13
D. 17, 43, 84, 3
E. 9, 2, 10, 41
F. 24, 46, 20, 11

Page Eighty-five
A. 5, 2
B. 5, 4
C. 4, 6
D. 4, 8

Page Eighty-six
A. 3, 6
B. 8, 4

Page Eighty-seven
A. 45, 49, 50
B. 96, 93, 92
C. 30, 60, 80
D. 20, 25, 35, 40
E. 60, 45, 40, 35
F. 8, 12, 16, 18
G. 5, 7, 17, 19
H. 21, 61, 81
I. 60, 50, 30, 20
J. 22, 16, 14

Page Eighty-eight
A. 7, 5, 4, 2, 1
B. 59, 62, 63, 64
C. 20, 40, 90
D. 40, 50, 55,
E. 70, 50, 40, 20
F. 6, 10, 14, 16
G. 80, 65, 60, 55
H. 300, 700, 800
I. 7, 11, 21
J. 64, 34, 14

Page Eighty-nine
A. 2   C. 4
B. 2   D. 4

Page Ninety-one
A. 8 cm   D. 2 cm
B. 10 cm   E. 4 cm
C. 3 cm

Page Ninety-two
A. 2   G. 4
B. 9   H. 3
C. 6   I. 10
D. 8   J. 1
E. 12   K. 7
F. 5   L. 11

Page Ninety-four
1. Monkey
2. Bear
3. Elephant